GLASSH

Fiona Grant

SHIRE PUBLICATIONS

Published in Great Britain in 2013 by Shire Publications Ltd, Midland House, West Way, Botley, Oxford OX2 0PH, United Kingdom.

43-01 21st Street, Suite 220B, Long Island City, NY 11101, USA.

E-mail: shire@shirebooks.co.uk   www.shirebooks.co.uk

A CIP catalogue record for this book is available from the British Library.

Shire Library no. 747.   ISBN-13: 978 0 74781 246 3

Fiona Grant has asserted her right under the Copyright, Designs and Patents Act, 1988, to be identified as the author of this book.

Designed by Tony Truscott Designs, Sussex, UK and typeset in Perpetua and Gill Sans.

Printed in China through Worldprint Ltd.

13 14 15 16 17   10 9 8 7 6 5 4 3 2 1

COVER IMAGE
The palm house at Bicton Botanical Gardens, Devon, an iron and glass domed structure most likely built by D. & E. Bailey in the early Victorian period.

TITLE PAGE IMAGE
A group in Victorian dress sitting on the steps to the entrance of the domed conservatory at Weston Park, built by Jones & Clark c. 1841.

CONTENTS PAGE IMAGE
A three-quarter span glasshouse from the Richardson & Company catalogue (early twentieth century), showing their 'patent system' of roof ventilation.

ACKNOWLEDGEMENTS
I would like to thank the people who have allowed me to use illustrations, which are acknowledged as follows:

Acanthus Holden, page 60 (top); Susannah & Graham Alcorn, page 57 (bottom); Archives and Heritage Birmingham City Library, pages 29 (bottom), 32 (bottom); Belfast City Council, page 33; Dr Stephen Briggs, page 41 (bottom); Margaret Broadey, page 47 (right); Jim Buckland, page 59 (top); Marian Byrne, page 64; Susan Campbell, pages 19 (top), 23, 40 (top), 41 (top); City of Westminster Archives Centre, page 28; Chris Cronin, page 65 (top); Steven Desmond, contents page; The Fitzwilliam Museum, University of Cambridge / The Bridgeman Art Library, page 22; Dan Fisk, page 62 (both); Francis Frith Collection, page 53; Andrew Fuller, front cover and pages 38, 49; Garden Museum, pages 10, 13, 30, 37, 40 (bottom), 44 (top), 66; Dr Ulli Harding, page 58; Ian Harris, page 34; Simon Harrison, page 65 (bottom); Anthony Herbert, pages 45, 47 (left), 51; Edward James Foundation, page 54; Mary Evans Picture Library, pages 11, 18; A. McArthur and www.picturethepast.co.uk page 5; Jeremy Milln, page 63; RHS Lindley Library, pages 8, 16, 20; Eddie Ross, page 24; Chris Sawyer, pages 12, 39 (both); Shropshire Archives, page 31; Trevor Sims, page 59 (bottom); The Stapleton Collection / The Bridgeman Art Library, page 9; Weston Park Foundation, title page.

All other illustrations are from the author's collection.

Shire Publications is supporting the Woodland Trust, the UK's leading woodland conservation charity, by funding the dedication of trees.

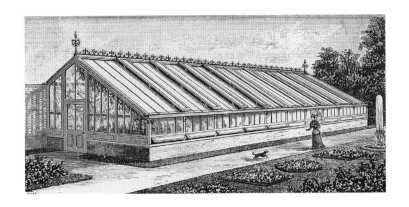

CONTENTS

INTRODUCTION

THE RANGE OF EXOTIC PLANTS introduced by travellers and explorers from around the globe increased dramatically in the seventeenth and eighteenth centuries. The desire to cultivate these wonderful rarities fired man's imagination into inventing ingenious methods of growing them in northen Europe's harsher climate. These early structures were often crude, designed merely to protect the tender exotics from frost, but over time more sophisticated structures were developed.

The introduction of oranges via Spain led to the development of the orangery, a substantial structure, initially ill-lit and thick-walled, which was not ideal for the cultivation of plants. Pineapples from South America presented a greater challenge; for them sunken pits called 'pine stoves' or 'pineries' were devised, which were heated with steaming manure or spent tanners' bark.

The eighteenth century was a period of experimentation. Structures evolved by trial and error; successful designs were then published by the head gardeners or architects who had devised them. These designs were clearly illustrated with plans and furnished with descriptions of structures they had built for their aristocratic clients, so that they could be copied and built by the landowner's own estate staff. Because of the cost of materials, particularly glass, and the intensive labour required to maintain them, these structures were limited to the wealthiest landowners.

During the Industrial Revolution new materials and technologies were introduced, which brought down the costs of both materials and manufacture, making glasshouses affordable to the emerging middle classes. Prices fell even more drastically when developments in glassmaking made possible larger, and cheaper, panes of glass, and in 1845 the tax on glass was abolished. From then onwards scores of manufacturers emerged, describing themselves as 'horticultural builders', to cater for this new market. A range of buildings was on offer, in both timber and iron, suitable for a variety of different crops: vineries, peach houses, tomato and fig houses. Ornamental plants were also provided for, in order to satisfy the craze for exotic blooms such as orchids arriving from South America, India and South Africa. Plants from temperate regions, such as grapes and peaches, were forced into early production, to provide out-of-season fruit throughout the year. Shade-loving ferns and sun-seeking chrysanthemums also had their own, specially designed houses.

These nineteenth and early twentieth century structures reflect the peak of Victorian ingenuity, a combination of clever design and innovative technology. They represent the care and consideration paid to the most humble and functional of objects, so typical of that century. This remarkable attention to detail, from ingenious ventilation mechanisms to decorative ironwork, combined to create a satisfying blend of function and beauty. The range of crops these structures nurtured throughout the season is a testimony not only to the ingenuity of the manufacturers who built them, but also to the skill of the gardeners who assiduously tended the plants, persuading them to grow and flourish far from their natural environment.

A painting
by A. McArthur
of the interior of
the camellia house
at Wollaton Hall,
Nottingham,
grade II*,
built in 1823
by Jones & Clark.

THE ORANGERY

The orange garden is very fine, and leads into the greenhouse, at the end of which is a hall to eat in, and the conservatory some hundred feet long, adorned with maps.

John Evelyn's *Diary* (10 September, 1677).

CITRUS FRUITS were cultivated by the Persians as long ago as the fifth century AD. They were prized not only for their scent and beauty, but also for their medicinal and culinary qualities. The bitter orange, *Citrus aurantium bigaradia*, and the lemon, *Citrus limonium*, both natives of south-eastern China and northern Burma, were the first citrus trees introduced to Europe. It is thought that the Arabs introduced the plants around the thirteenth century to the southern Mediterranean and Moorish Spain, hence the current name for the bitter orange, the Seville.

Citrus trees were being cultivated in Italy by the fifteenth century. The trees were usually grown in large pots to be displayed on terraces and steps, and were well suited to the architectural style of the Italian Renaissance. Although these species are hardier than the sweet orange, some protection was still needed in the winter months, except in the most southerly Mediterranean regions. At the end of the summer the trees would be brought into shelter of some kind, such as garden rooms or grottoes, or into open galleries under a terrace, which could then be enclosed with wooden shutters. There they remained until the spring, when they were once more brought outside to stand in the sun.

From the mid-sixteenth century orange seeds from Italy were brought into northern European countries such as Germany, Flanders, France and England. In the north the trees tended to be planted directly into the ground, perhaps in the shelter of a south-facing wall. However, further protection was needed, and temporary or semi-permanent wooden structures, first developed in Germany in the early seventeenth century, were built around them. A framework of timber was boarded with wooden panels that could be gradually removed as the weather warmed up in the spring. In order

Opposite:
The raised central section of the orangery at Margam Park, built by Anthony Keck between 1786 and 1790, ornamented with garlands and *bucrania*, or bulls' skulls, carved in relief, topped with four urns.

Above:
An engraving showing a wooden structure in the process of being built over orange trees planted both in pots and in the ground. From *Hesperides* by J. B. Ferrari, 1670.

to keep the temperature above freezing, some kind of heating was required. In particularly cold weather charcoal braziers were strategically placed to maintain a temperature of around 40–45 degrees.

Sir Francis Carew, a courtier to Queen Elizabeth I, is said to have been the first Englishman to grow orange trees successfully by using this method. They were planted into the ground at his estate in Beddington, Surrey, and were sheltered during the winter months in a long wooden structure built around them, heated by two stoves. Over a hundred years later the trees were described as still flourishing and producing large quantities of fruit.

As the fashion for Italian gardens spread north, the practice of growing citrus trees in pots became increasingly popular, since it complemented the new architectural style: the trees could be positioned to give colour and height to the garden. This further encouraged the use of permanent structures, since trees in pots were portable and easily moved inside in winter and outside in summer. The first permanent structures dedicated to over-wintering the plants had solid roofs, with narrow windows providing the only light. Heating was still provided in the coldest months by charcoal braziers; a Dutch innovation was the use of fixed stoves burning either coal or charcoal, although this system inevitably gave an uneven distribution of heat. Another solution was to employ a garden boy to pull a brazier on wheels up and down the length of the room. However, it was soon recognised that the smoke from these methods was detrimental to the health of the plants. Attempts to provide heat by means of a hypocaust, a system of under-floor flues, were pioneered in the late seventeenth century, and the method was developed throughout the next century to become the norm.

Top: Interior of a Dutch orangery, 1676. The citrus trees, arranged in rows, are planted in both tubs and pots. The only source of light is the small windows in the front wall. Two stoves provide heat. The two men in the background are carrying a tree outside. Bottom: A lemon, fig and orange tree in wooden tubs, from Jan van der Groen, *Den Netherlantsen Hovenier*.

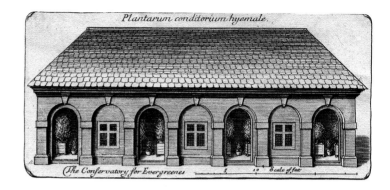

The Conservatory for Evergreens at the Oxford Physic Garden, from a plan of 1675. The conservatory was built in 1621. It was 60 feet long, unheated, with a tiled roof, and small windows alternating with open archways. Although the building was intended for a collection of evergreens, orange trees in tubs can be made out alongside other plants.

The word 'orangeries' was not yet applied to the permanent structures for the protection of citrus trees and other tender exotics; this term was initially used at the time to describe either a collection of orange trees, or the area where the trees were displayed outdoors in the summer. In England the word 'greenhouse', first used by John Evelyn in 1664, referred to a building for over-wintering tender evergreens such as bay, myrtle, pomegranates and of course citrus trees. The term 'conservatory' was also used, since the plants were conserved, rather than grown, during the winter months.

The orangery increasingly became an architectural feature in its own right, with scant regard given to the horticultural requirements of the trees; since they were required merely to survive the winter, their growing conditions were not considered critical. The magnificent orangery at Versailles, built by Mansart in 1685, whilst as huge as one would expect – over 500 feet long with wings at either end – was essentially a vaulted gallery with a rusticated façade built under a garden terrace, echoing the Italian practice of over-wintering citrus trees in galleries. An important innovation at Versailles was the use of large wooden boxes, rather than terracotta pots, as containers for the trees. The 'Versailles tubs', as they became known, had hinged doors for ease of cultivation, and rings where poles could be inserted, so that they could be carried by two men in the manner of a sedan chair.

In England the fashion for the cultivation of oranges was given a further boost when William III was crowned king in 1689. William, a member of the House of Orange in the Dutch republic, ruled jointly with his wife Mary, the daughter of James II. Both keen horticulturalists, they were able to draw on Dutch expertise for the latest structural developments in horticulture. Since oranges were the symbol of the House of Orange, it is not surprising that they had a large collection of orange trees. Dutch experts were brought over to construct three stove houses (so called from the method of heating them) at Hampton Court Palace, in which to house the oranges and the royal collection of other exotics. Plans and elevations published around 1701 of one of these

A mature orange tree planted in a tub at Versailles, reputedly the oldest orange tree in France at that time. The figures give an idea of scale. From *Le Magasin Pittoresque*, 1857.

stovehouses, which were built in the latest Dutch fashion, show a tiled roof, with sloping glass casements on the south-facing side. From the Duchess of Beaufort, herself a keen gardener, we learn that each was 55 feet long but only 8 feet wide, each with two fireplaces heating the under-floor vaults. Designed more for the cultivation of exotic plants than for the over-wintering of citrus, they were arguably influential in the design of hothouses in the eighteenth century. The stoves were demolished after Mary's death in 1694, and a more classical orangery, in the form of a brick wing to the palace, was built by Sir Christopher Wren towards the end of the century, and this is the structure that we still see there today, now known as the Lower Orangery.

In eighteenth-century England the development of the greenhouse, or orangery as it was now beginning to be known, was driven by the passion for cultivating the new plants being introduced from Britain's colonies, and North America in particular. Wealthy collectors built them to house their collections of exotic plants in the manner of outdoor 'cabinets of curiosity'. At the turn of the century some orangeries were built as arcaded galleries, echoing the terraces of Italy, with glass windows, rather than shutters, built into the arches. They were often built as extensions to the house, as mentioned earlier at Hampton Court, and also at Dyrham Park (William Talman, 1701), Kensington Palace (Nicholas Hawksmoor, 1704), and Blenheim Palace (Sir John Vanbrugh, 1704).

As the century progressed, orangeries became separated from the mansion, coinciding with the influence of the landscape movement, which did away with formal gardens to create a seemingly more natural environment. The newly landscaped grounds were enhanced with a range of garden buildings reflecting the current fashion in classical architecture. Architects such as Robert Adam (Croome Court, 1760), William Chambers (Kew Gardens, 1761) and James Paine (Temple of Diana, Weston Park, *c.* 1760) used the classical style to create orangeries as 'temples in the landscape'.

The orangery at Heveningham Hall, Suffolk, by Samuel Wyatt, *c.* 1760. The large windows admit ample light, but the glazed roof was a nineteenth-century addition. The columns, balustrading and pilasters are of wood and plaster.

Whilst the benefits of light for the growth of plants had been recognised earlier in the century, improvements were slow to develop; since the trees were dormant during the winter, growth was not the primary consideration. However, Richard Bradley, Professor of Botany at Cambridge, concerned by the poor health of the citrus trees he had seen, caused by the lack of light and ventilation in buildings where horticultural requirements were sacrificed for style, wrote in 1720 that 'the greenhouses as they are commonly built serve more for ornament than to use'. He collaborated with an Italian architect, Galilei, to conceive an attractive design that also provided a more amenable environment for the trees. Gradually, over the century, windows became larger to let in more light, often being sash windows from floor to ceiling, with shutters for insulation. These could be completely removed in summer to create a loggia for entertainment, thus providing the buildings with a dual purpose.

Towards the end of the eighteenth century many landowners owned huge collections of orange and lemon trees, and orangeries increased in size in order to accommodate them. The magnificent orangery at Margam Park in South Wales was built for Thomas Mansel Talbot between 1786 and 1790 to house his collection of over one hundred trees. Plants were arranged in the central, heated gallery lit by twenty-seven tall, arched windows. At each end was a pavilion, one containing his collection of statues, and the other his library; thus the building housed three different collections in the manner of a cabinet of curiosity. The huge door at the back gives some idea of the size of the trees:

A postcard of c. 1910 showing the interior of the orangery at Margam Park. The citrus trees are planted in large wooden tubs arranged in a row at the back. Other tender exotics are placed along the front wall.

an observer in 1878 described them as being between 12 and 18 feet high. Many of them were the originals, reputedly a gift from the king of Spain to Queen Elizabeth I. The story goes that the ship transporting them became stranded on the shore at Margam and therefore its contents became the property of the lord of the manor. In the summer the trees, in square tubs 4 feet wide and 3 feet deep, were displayed on the terrace in front of the building, and must have made a fine sight, alongside the pools, fountains and statuary.

The glazing of orangery roofs became increasingly common in the nineteenth century and was standard practice by the end of the century. This came about not only from a greater understanding of the benefits of light on plants, but also perhaps from the use of modern materials such as cast and wrought iron, which made such structures feasible. As the century progressed, the orangery gradually gave way to the more fashionable conservatory. The terms 'greenhouse' and 'conservatory' had been largely interchangeable throughout most of the eighteenth century, but the meanings began to diverge towards the end: a greenhouse was for conserving and over-wintering 'greens', that is evergreens; a conservatory was a glass-roofed structure providing more suitable growing conditions for the plants, both temporary and permanent. In the nineteenth century conservatories became increasingly popular, often linked to the house in the manner of an 'outdoor room',

The orangery at Margam Park is now used as a venue for weddings and other functions, reflecting the eighteenth-century practice of using orangeries as places for entertainment after the trees had been removed in the summer.

The orangery at Heath House, Tean, Staffordshire, was built to a design by James Trubshaw c. 1830. It has a curved glass and iron roof and overlooks a sunken Victorian garden.

eventually superseding the orangery as the high-status garden building. This new fashion caused an observer to comment that 'a mania for conservatories has spread contagiously among all the richer classes … they are attached to all the more pretentious houses'.

An unusual iron and glass conservatory or orangery at Hopton Court, Shropshire, with a curved roof. It is built against a hot-wall, and was most likely built in the 1830s or 1840s.

Plate 25.

A PINERY & ORANGERY.

Executed for
JOHN WALTER, Esqr.
Teddington,
Middx.

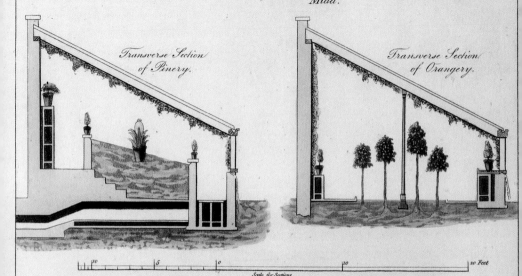

Transverse Section of Pinery.

Transverse Section of Orangery.

20   5   0   20   20 Feet

Scale for Sections.

Elevation.

Plan.

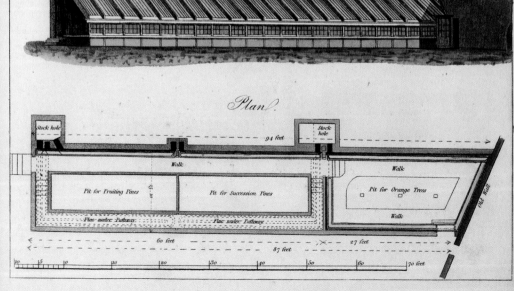

Stock hole

Stock hole

94 feet

Walk

Walk

Pit for Fruiting Pines

Pit for Succession Pines

Pit for Orange Trees

Flue under Pathway

Flue under Pathway

Walk

Old Wall

60 feet

27 feet

87 feet

10   15   10   10   20   30   40   50   60   70 feet

London, Published Septr. 1st. 1806. by J. Taylor, 59. High Holborn.

AN AGE OF EXPERIMENTATION

As of late years there have been great quantities of curious exotic plants introduced into the English garden so the number of greenhouses or conservatories has increased, and not only a greater skill in the management and ordering of these plants therewith, but also a greater knowledge of the structure and contrivance of these places so as to render them both useful and ornamental hath been acquired…

Philip Miller, *The Gardener's Dictionary* (1752).

THE NEED for more sophisticated forms of glasshouse in the eighteenth century was stimulated by the new range of exotic introductions to Britain. For, unlike citrus trees, which were dormant in winter, these plants needed warmer conditions throughout the year in order to achieve optimum growth. Consequently, greater consideration was given to both light and heat in order to create the appropriate environment.

The Dutch had developed a new type of structure in the 1680s, a kind of lean-to arrangement, quite narrow, with glass casements sloping from the wall to the ground. In some cases there was a narrow 'roof' of wood or other opaque material. Heating was supplied by under-floor flues. This was the type built at Hampton Court for Queen Mary. Such structures were first known as 'stoves' because of the method of heating them, but by the mid-eighteenth century they were also called 'hothouses'. Both terms implied heated structures for the cultivation of tropical and subtropical plants, rather than the cooler greenhouse or conservatory. A wealthy Dutch cloth merchant, Pieter de la Court, had experimented with various forms of stoves for cultivating exotics in the seventeenth century. His methods of construction, along with illustrations, were published much later, in 1737, thus disseminating his ideas throughout Europe.

Philip Miller, curator of the Botanic Garden of the Society of Apothecaries, now the Chelsea Physic Garden, was a key figure in pioneering new horticultural techniques throughout the eighteenth century in England.

Opposite: cross-section, elevation and ground plan of a combined pinery and orangery. The pinery has two beds, one for 'succession' pineapples (at the intermediate stage) and the other for fruiting. Grapevines are grown alongside the pineapples, trained under the glass roof.

He had visited de la Court in Holland, who no doubt had a strong influence on the stoves that Miller built at Chelsea. In the first edition (1731) of Philip Miller's *Gardener's Dictionary*, a plate shows two stove houses with solid roofs on either side of his greenhouse; but in a later edition (1752) they are depicted

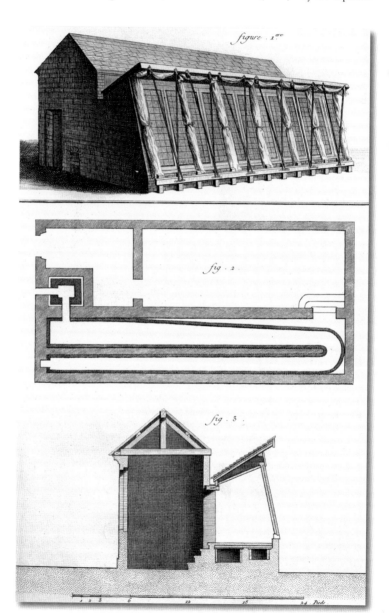

Right: An illustration from Diderot's *Encyclopaedia*, 1760, showing a hothouse built against a shed that contains the furnace for heating the subterranean hot-air flues. The glass is angled to catch the sun. The blinds protect the plants in cold weather.

Opposite, top: Elevation and ground plan of the greenhouse and two stoves in the Chelsea Physic Garden. Published in Philip Miller's *Gardener's Dictionary* (1752), this shows the stoves or hothouses with glazed roofs. The two hot-walls behind the stoves are shown in section.

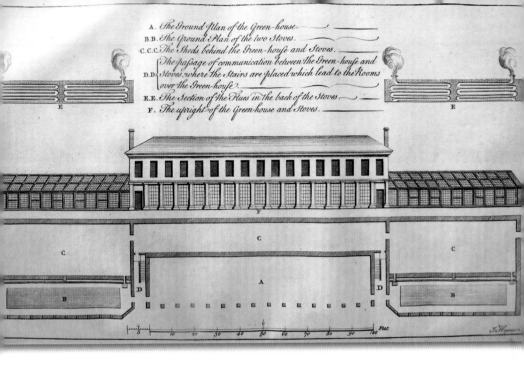

A. The Ground Plan of the Green-house.
B.B. The Ground Plan of the two Stoves.
C.C.C. The Sheds behind the Green-house and Stoves.
D.D. The passage of communication between the Green-house and Stoves, where the Stairs are placed which lead to the Rooms over the Green-house.
E.E. The Section of the Flues in the back of the Stoves.
F. The upright of the Green-house and Stoves.

with glass roofs. This was a key development, designed not only to admit more light, but also to ensure that there were two opportunities for the sun to strike the glass vertically, the most favourable angle. Miller's stoves were built against 'hot-walls', hollow walls containing a serpentine flue that led from a firegrate at the bottom of the wall to a chimney at the top.

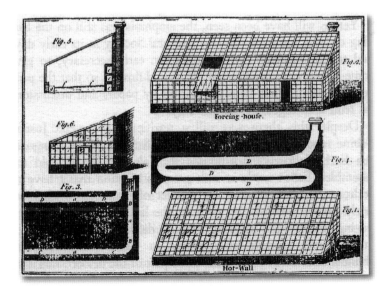

A forcing house shown in elevation and sections, with a ground plan demonstrating the arrangement of the flues. The sloping lean-to house is heated by the hot-wall shown in section. From J. Abercrombie's *The Gardeners' Daily Assistant*, 1786.

Later in the century the flues were built proud of the back wall, so as to throw more heat into the house. The next step was to make the flues completely freestanding so that the heat could be distributed more efficiently to where it was most needed, usually around the sides and along the front of the house. Hot-air flues were not ideal, however, for there was the constant threat of leaks letting dangerous fumes into the house; it was also difficult to maintain a constant temperature with this system, which needed frequent attendance.

Because of these heating methods, eighteenth-century glasshouses were generally lean-to structures with low, glazed front walls on masonry foundations and with sloping glass roofs, made up of frames of small panes of glass set between closely spaced timber glazing bars. Between 1746 and 1845 glass was taxed by weight, which made it extremely expensive and encouraged manufacturers to make glass for horticultural purposes as thin as possible, as little as $^1/_{16}$ inch (1–2 mm). The panes therefore had to be small

A range of hothouses, including a greenhouse, and a peach and vine house where the peaches are trained against a trellis on the back wall, from J. Abercrombie's *The Gardeners' Daily Assistant,* 1786.

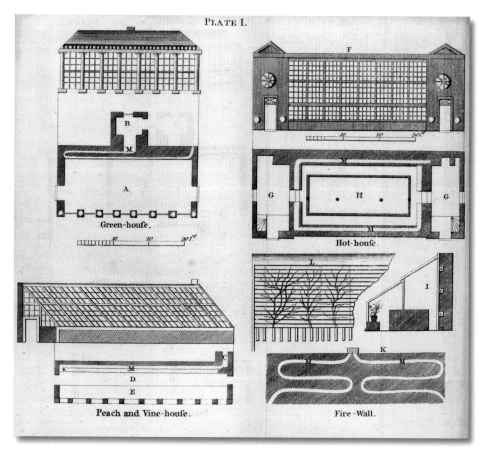

PLATE I.

Green-houfe.

Hot-houfe.

Peach and Vine-houfe.

Fire-Wall.

since the glass was too fragile for larger ones. The panes usually measured 6x6 or 6x8 inches. At this time two types of glass were produced: crown glass and cylinder glass. Crown glass was more expensive, so sparingly used in horticulture. Cylinder glass was the cheaper option; it was blown into a cylinder, which was then cut open and flattened into a sheet before being cut into panes.

Ventilation was achieved with sliding frames at the top of the roof, designed to slide down the roof in the manner of a sash window. They were operated either by a winding mechanism of cords or chains, or counterbalanced with a heavy material such as lead. The lower lights could also be opened: either a casement hinged at the top and propped open with a latch, or made of two frames, one of which could be opened by sliding sideways.

More than any other, the exotic introduction that drove the design of hothouses was the pineapple, which arrived in Europe from South America in the sixteenth century. Its bizarre appearance and unique flavour caused a sensation, inciting the desire to grow it in Europe. However, the pineapple being a native of tropical Brazil, great ingenuity was required to discover a method of cultivation suitable for the harsher climate of northern Europe.

The pineapple was first successfully grown and ripened in the Netherlands, where the remarkable properties of tan bark were discovered, in the late seventeenth century. Tan bark, or tanners' bark, is the waste from the oak bark used in the leather tanning process and has the ability to heat up and retain its heat for a considerable time. Pineapples were initially grown in pit houses, essentially 'hot beds' lined with brick, sunk about 4 feet into the ground for greater insulation, and roofed with glass. The beds were filled with warm, moist fermenting tan bark, and the pineapples, grown in pots, were plunged into it. Further heat could be provided with hot-air flues, or in some cases, as at Heligan, with manure piled up around the pit.

By the eighteenth century this technology had transferred to Britain, and the ability to grow pineapples became a status symbol: a deep purse and a skilful gardener were

Plan, elevation and section of a stove, designed to hold one hundred fruiting pineapples. The lean-to stove is built against a hot-wall heated by two firegrates. The pineapples are grown in pots buried in a bed of tan bark. From T. Hitt, *The Modern Gardener*, 1771.

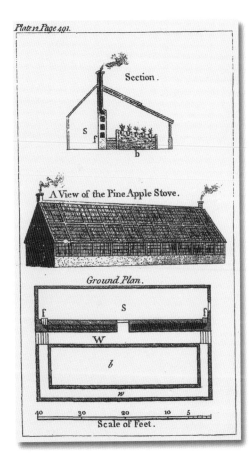

Plate 12 Page 491.

Section.

A View of the Pine Apple Stove.

Ground Plan.

Scale of Feet.

needed, since a pineapple took at least two years to mature, requiring heat in the range of 70 to 80 degrees. The first person believed to have grown one successfully in Britain was Sir Matthew Decker, a Dutchman, as was his gardener, Henry Telende. He was so proud of this achievement that he had a 'portrait' painted of his pineapple in 1720.

Because pineapples took so long to mature, they needed specific requirements at different stages of their development. It was therefore recommended that they were given a variety of growing conditions, by providing a range of different structures. For example, small low pine pits were required for the early stages of growth, and larger, warmer pine stoves were needed for the growing on and ripening of the fruit. However, this was the ideal, and most establishments had to make do with stoves divided into two or three compartments that could then be heated to different temperatures, thereby providing the growing conditions appropriate to each stage of growth.

A description of 1781 suggested that a pine stove should be between 12 and 14 feet in width in order to allow for a large central bed about 6 to 8 feet wide, in which the pineapples were grown. These beds were usually higher at the back than at the front, in order to provide a sloping surface paralleling

Painting of a pineapple, by Theodore Netscher, 1720, to commemorate Sir Matthew Decker's success in ripening the fruit. The inscription reads: 'To the eternal memory of Matthew Decker, Baronet, and Theodore Netscher, Gentleman. This pineapple deemed worthy of the Royal table, grew at Richmond at the cost of the former and still seems to grow by the art of the latter.'

the slope of the glass above, so that all the plants were at the same distance from the glass. It could be any length from 20 to 100 feet, depending on the number of pineapples to be grown. William Speechly, gardener to the Duke of Portland at Welbeck Abbey, built a pine stove 250 feet long, which was later described as the first of such a size erected in Britain.

Stoves and hothouses were initially developed for the cultivation of exotics – plants from tropical and subtropical climates. Once this had been achieved, attention turned to less demanding plants that had hitherto been grown outside. The focus was now on forcing early and out-of-season crops, in order to produce, with careful management, a succession of ripe fruit throughout most of the year.

Vines for dessert grapes had previously been grown outside against walls, heated or not, and in some cases against sloping banks. With pine stoves well established, vines could now share the space with the pineapples; this was achieved by planting the vine outside the pine stove, inserting the rod, or stem, of the vine through a hole in the front wall, and training it up under the roof. Apart from the obvious economies of heating, the vine also provided shade for the pineapples below. This structure later became known as a 'pinery-vinery'. However, the system did not win universal approval, as the two plants have essentially different requirements, the pineapple, originally from the tropics, requiring humid conditions, and the vine, from the Mediterranean, preferring a drier atmosphere. It was not until the end of the eighteenth century that the vinery, a house dedicated to the cultivation of dessert grapes, emerged.

There was no standard design for glasshouses in the eighteenth century, causing the horticulturalist Thomas Andrew Knight to comment that 'internally two are hardly ever constructed alike, though intended for the same purpose'. Gardeners, and to some extent architects, developed their own hothouses and stoves based on practical experience. These designs were often published, and the structures were described in some detail for others to follow, in the manner of pattern books. These structures could then be built by estate staff. William Speechly wrote two treatises, one on the cultivation of the vine and another on the pineapple, with ground plans and sections of his recommended structures. Architects such as William Robertson and James Shaw published splendid folios of examples of their work, from orangeries to peach houses, built for their various clients.

Section of a pine and grape stove, showing the vine trained up under the roof to provide shade for the pineapples, which are grown in two beds or pits. The darker rectangles indicate the flues. William Speechly, *A Treatise on the Culture of the Pineapple*, 1796.

EARLY IRON-FRAMED GLASSHOUSES

It is impossible to give an idea, by any verbal description, of the lightness of elegance of these Horticultural Buildings; their seemingly airy and unsubstantial form produces in the eye of the spectator at first glance, a magic-like effect, which, on a nearer inspection, is absorbed in the feeling of amazement at the real strength and firmness of the several buildings, announcing a durability to which no limit can be assigned.

The Gardener's Magazine, Vol. 3, 1837.

IRON was very much the 'new' material at the turn of the century; improvements in the manufacture of cast iron had led to its use as a constructional building material by the end of the eighteenth century. As early as 1803, the fashionable landscape designer Humphry Repton was recommending its use for garden buildings, and for conservatories in particular. Such a strong and durable material was ideal for creating glass structures: iron can be cast in shapes that are difficult and expensive to achieve in wood, and the structural components, being slighter than timber, let in more light. Iron also offered greater decorative possibilities than wood, hitherto the chief material used in the construction of hothouses.

As the Industrial Revolution gathered pace in the early nineteenth century, developments in science and technology were reflected in the design of glasshouses. An increasingly scientific approach to horticulture led to a greater understanding of the requirements of cultivated plants, such as an appreciation of the effect on them of sunlight. There was much discussion concerning the optimum angle of glasshouse roofs in order to maximise the benefit of the sun's rays. Improvements in the production of iron had established it as a viable alternative to timber, and this engendered much debate concerning the relative values of timber and iron. In 1816 the eminent horticultural writer John Claudius Loudon developed a wrought-iron glazing bar, with a more slender profile than cast iron, only ½ inch wide, which could be formed into curved bars to create an elegant curvilinear structure.

Opposite: Detail of iron-framed palm house at Bicton (see cover illustration) showing the narrow glazing bars and the overlapping, small panes of glass.

This was an attempt to improve the appearance of hothouses, which he described as 'offensive to the eye' with their 'lean-to shed-looking glass roofs'. Loudon was also responding to a theory proposed by Sir George Mackenzie, who in 1815 suggested that a curvilinear roof created the optimum angle for maximum exposure to the sun. Moreover, the narrower iron glazing bars admitted more light than their wooden counterparts, an important consideration at a time when glass was very expensive, and small panes 6 inches wide were the most economical size. In his enthusiasm to promote both the material and the curvilinear shape, Loudon had several hothouses constructed at his property in Bayswater, London, in 1818, to demonstrate the range of forms made possible with iron.

These structures were built by W. & D. Bailey, of Holborn, London. William and Daniel Bailey were already established in the iron and brass trade, and in the same year Loudon transferred to them the rights for his glazing bar, which they patented in January 1819. The Baileys then went on to construct elegant curvilinear iron-framed structures for a number of clients. Twenty-two are listed in Loudon's *Encyclopaedia of Gardening* (1822), including a pine stove for the eminent horticulturalist Thomas Andrew Knight of Downton Castle, a camellia house for the famous Loddiges Nursery of Hackney, and two stoves for the Horticultural Society (later the Royal Horticultural Society). These clients were at the forefront of horticultural developments at this time and therefore reflect the esteem in which such structures were held.

A design for a quarter-sphere curvilinear glasshouse by W. & D. Bailey for Lord St Vincent at Rochetts, Brentwood, Essex, c. 1824, based on Sir George Mackenzie's designs and using Loudon's wrought-iron glazing bar.

In 1827 the Baileys built a freestanding domed glasshouse for Mrs Beaumont at Bretton Hall, West Yorkshire, a daring design since a freestanding circular structure had never before been built. The only structural support came from the wrought-iron sash bars and eight cast-iron columns. It was reported that when it was erected, and before it was glazed, 'the slightest wind put the whole of it in motion from the base to the summit', but that once it was glazed 'it was found to be perfectly firm and strong'. It must have been quite a sight, measuring 100 feet in diameter, 60 feet high, and topped with a gilt coronet. The low wall on which it rested was also made of iron, in which ventilation shutters were placed. Further ventilation was provided by an opening skylight underneath the coronet, and windows that opened inwardly between the upper and lower domes. It was

A derelict cast-iron domed glasshouse at Hilton Hall, Staffordshire, awaits restoration. The quality of the iron castings decorated with key-friezes and palmettes justifies its Grade I listing. While its history is not yet known, it was most likely built in the 1830s.

heated with steam-filled pipes, the most up-to-date method at the time, but in such a tall structure the heat rose to the top, causing significant discrepancies in the distribution of heat. Unfortunately the structure was dismantled and sold on Mrs Beaumont's death in 1832, possibly because it had proved uneconomical. It was probably intended as a palm house, because its height would have accommodated not only palm trees, but also a variety of tall tropical plants such as banana, guava and sugar cane. Collecting these dramatic plants and showcasing them in large houses was generally the

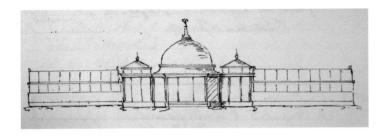

Sketch from the Jones & Clark order book for a large conservatory with a central dome for the Earl of Bradford at Weston Park, Staffordshire, dated 1840. (See title page picture).

province of the botanic gardens – but they would have brought significant status to those private collectors wealthy enough to own them.

The Palm House at Bicton Park Botanical Gardens, Devon, is a remarkable survival of the Baileys' work. The precise date of its construction is not known, but it was most likely built by the next generation of Baileys, Daniel and Edward, who were known to be working in the 1830s and 1840s. Unlike the dome at Bretton, it is a lean-to structure, with the supporting wall rendered 'invisible' by closely following the outline of the building. It has a large half-dome protruding from the rectangular central section, with two smaller quarter-domes on either side, measuring about 68 feet in length and 33 feet at its widest. Eighteen thousand small panes of glass overlap between the wrought-iron ribs; the ribs decrease in number towards the centre, thus avoiding congestion. There are ventilation flaps along the ridge and in the back wall. It still contains palm trees today.

Mrs Beaumont of Bretton Hall was clearly a keen plant collector, with a wide range of the latest glasshouses in which to house her plants. Only two years after the domed conservatory was built for her, she ordered a large iron-framed heath house and a greenhouse from John Jones & Company of Birmingham. Not much is known of Jones, though Loudon rated him highly, calling him 'decidedly the best hothouse builder in Britain' (1831). Jones was the son of the gardener to the Earl of Aylesford, so he may have well brought the horticultural expertise to the partnership, formed in 1818, with Thomas Clark, the son of an iron-founder, also from Birmingham. Jones & Clark quickly established themselves as one of the foremost manufacturers of metallic hothouses in the country, and by 1832 they could boast of having constructed

Opposite:
The original sketch for the domed conservatory at Bretton Hall, West Yorkshire, by the Baileys, undated. The coronet, as built, is sketched in to the left. The ventilation shutters can be seen in the parapet wall.

The conservatory at Bretton Hall, as erected in 1827. The entrance porch appears wider than in the original sketch. J. C. Loudon *An Encyclopaedia of Cottage, Farm and Villa Architecture*, 1839.

Opposite: Plan for a metallic hothouse (1828), by Jones & Clark for the Earl of Powis at Walcot Hall, Shropshire, showing cross-sections of the rafter and copper sash bar. Light no. 2 is glazed with their innovative 'circular perforated laps'.

The conservatory at The Grange, Northington, Hampshire, built for Alexander Baring by Jones & Clark in 1824. The curved roofs over the pathways are made of two layers of iron, to protect against heat loss. Climbing plants are trained up the hollow columns.

over two hundred metallic hothouses. Their order book, dating from 1818 to 1858, lists a wide range of iron structures for hundreds of clients from all over Britain, making them one of the biggest suppliers of iron-framed glasshouses in the country.

An innovation regularly used by Jones & Clark was the use of copper for sash bars, rather than iron or wood; this was hailed by Loudon in 1813 as 'the greatest improvement hitherto made in horticultural architecture', since the resulting profile was even narrower than wrought iron, and the tubular underside provided some insulation.

The glasshouses entered in their order book for 1845 as 'two metallic hot-houses' miraculously survive in North Wales: they form a pair of lean-to vineries, each 36 feet long, on either side of a brick conservatory. Both have conventional sloping roofs of cast-iron rafters, supporting wooden lights about 3 feet wide, with copper sash bars and long narrow panes of crown glass. Ventilation was achieved with sliding sashes on the roof, each individually operated by its own winding mechanism, and the front casements are hinged at the top and operated manually with latches. Unusually, there are cast-iron openings for the vine rods built into the front wall, with iron rods attached to the roof for training the vines.

One of Jones & Clark's better-known surviving works is the conservatory at The Grange at Northington in Hampshire of 1824. It was later converted into a ballroom, and then, in the early twenty-first century, into a theatre. It was a magnificent and innovative structure, a rectangular building about

80 feet long and just under 50 feet wide, built to a design by the architect
C. R. Cockerell. Constructed in wrought and cast iron, it formed three
barrel-vaulted aisles separated by two glazed, ridged roofs. It was heated with
steam, and any attendant problems of condensation were mitigated by their

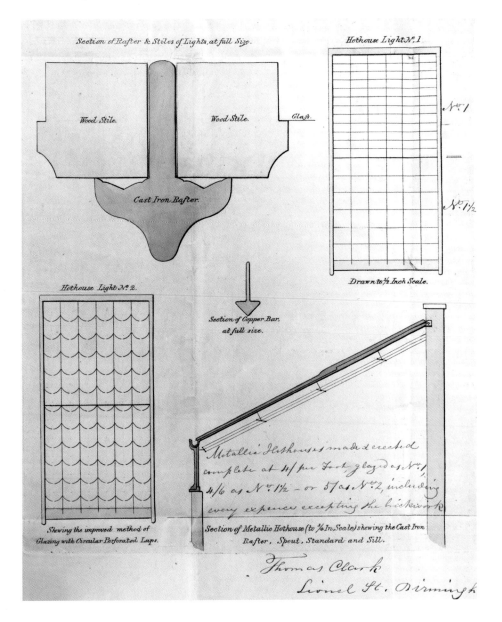

Section of Rafter & Stiles of Lights, at full Size.

Wood Stile.

Wood Stile.

Glass.

Cast Iron Rafter.

Hothouse Light Nº 1

Nº 1

Nº 1½

Drawn to ½ Inch Scale.

Hothouse Light Nº 2.

Section of Copper Bar.
at full size.

Shewing the improved method of
Glazing with Circular Perforated Laps.

Metallic Hothouses made & erected
complete at 4/ per Foot glazed as Nº 1
4/6 as Nº 1½ - or 5/ as Nº 2, including
every expence excepting the brickwork

Section of Metallic Hothouse (to ¾ In. Scale) shewing the Cast Iron
Rafter, Spout, Standard and Sill.

Thomas Clark
Lionel St. Birmingham

innovative method of glazing. Their 'circular perforated laps' were panes of glass shaped into a curve at the lower end, each having a tiny half-circle cut into it at the centre of the curve, which was designed to carry off the condensation from within the house. The cast-iron columns were hollow and acted as drainpipes, channelling the rainwater into a tank below ground level, thereby pre-dating Joseph Paxton's similar arrangement at Crystal Palace by decades. Cockerell further embellished the building by giving it the form of a classical temple with rendered columns and pilasters and a portico attached to the front.

By the 1850s John Jones had left the business. Clark later went into a partnership with Henry Hope and the firm became known as Clark & Hope. Hope became the sole owner in 1875. The company later merged with Crittall Windows Ltd to become Crittall Hope Ltd in 1965.

As at The Grange, many of the grander iron structures were built by hothouse makers in collaboration with an architect. The Irish ironmaster Richard Turner of Hammersmith Ironworks, Dublin, was in part responsible for several well-known structures. Probably the best-known is the Palm House at Kew, built in conjunction with the architect Decimus Burton between 1844 and 1848. Turner understood the inherent structural properties of wrought and cast iron and successfully combined them to create vast, spectacular structures that have stood the test of time. The curvilinear glasshouses Turner built in the botanic gardens of Ireland were effectively the prototypes of the structure at Kew. The Palm House in Belfast Botanic Garden was his first work, begun in 1839 to a design by Charles Lanyon.

A sketch of a range of three-quarter span glasshouses by Henry Hope, c. 1875. The two furthest have a banked-up outside bed, so are most likely vineries.

Turner was also responsible for the construction and design of the curvilinear range at Glasnevin, Dublin (National Botanic Gardens of Ireland), built between 1843 and 1848 but enlarged later in the century. It was fully restored in 1995.

Huge iron-framed glasshouses continued to be built, particularly in public gardens, where they were ideal for creating the impressive structures necessary to house large collections of plants, but for the private owner they began to fall out of favour around the middle of the nineteenth century. There were various drawbacks associated with iron, not least the initial cost, and because of its high conductivity heat loss was a serious problem, leading to greater heating expenses. Another problem was an increase in glass breakage due to the expansion and contraction of the iron, although this had been partly overcome with the use of copper glazing bars. However, after 1845, when the glass tax was abolished, the price of glass fell dramatically: larger panes of glass became cheaply available, and narrow glazing bars no longer held the advantage.

The palm house at Belfast Botanic Garden. The two wings were built by Richard Turner to a design by Charles Lanyon in the early 1840s. The central dome was added later.

THE PAXTON EFFECT

The glory of Chatsworth gardens, however, is the conservatory, a beautiful structure of glass and iron covering nearly an acre, the arched roof in the centre rising to a height of sixty-seven feet. In this famous hot-house are the rarest palms and tropical plants. It was designed by Joseph Paxton, the Duke's head gardener ...

Joel Cook, *England, Picturesque and Descriptive* (1882).

O N A MAY MORNING in 1826, a young man aged twenty-three arrived at Chatsworth House, Derbyshire, to begin his job as head gardener to the sixth Duke of Devonshire. His name was Joseph Paxton; he was to become one of the most respected horticulturalists of the nineteenth century and is still remembered today for his ground-breaking design for the Crystal Palace. His innovative approach to the construction of glasshouses moved the iron versus wood debate firmly forward in favour of wood.

On his arrival at Chatsworth there were a number of glasshouses already in use: four pine houses, two vineries, two peach houses and several cucumber frames, but no plant houses. When these structures had been repaired under Paxton's instructions, he turned his attention 'to the building and improvement of glass structures' and by 1830 Chatsworth had twenty-two hothouses as well as several pits and frames.

Paxton did not favour iron-framed houses, partly on the grounds of their initial cost, but also because of the problems with insulation and glass breakage. However, he had to acknowledge that their chief advantage was in allowing more light into the house; his experiments with timber structures, therefore, focused on designs that would admit as much, if not more, sunlight. His preference for timber brought him into conflict with that other major figure in horticulture, John Claudius Loudon, and so commenced what became an almost ideological battle between the virtues of iron versus timber. This was exacerbated when Paxton, like Loudon before him, launched several horticultural journals, including *The Magazine of Botany*

Opposite:
The interior of the Conservative Wall, a narrow glazed structure for protecting the peaches and camellias grown against the wall at Chatsworth House, Derbyshire.

The orchid house Paxton built at Chatsworth, an early experiment with a ridge-and-furrow roof. From Paxton's *Magazine of Botany*, 1836.

in 1834 and the popular weekly *Gardeners' Chronicle* in 1841. Within the pages of their respective journals the debate continued to rage.

Ironically, the structural feature for which Paxton is best-known – the ridge-and-furrow roof – was originally Loudon's idea (1817), but Paxton went on to refine it and to use it successfully in a number of buildings, culminating in the Crystal Palace for the Great Exhibition in 1851. The purpose of the ridge and furrow roof was to receive the sun's rays at a 90 degree angle twice a day; the ridges ran across the width of the house, and therefore the glazed sides of each ridge faced both east and west, the former catching the morning sun and the latter the afternoon sun. Rainwater drained into the 'furrow' or gully between the ridges, either into the usual guttering, or down hollow cast-iron columns, to be collected into tanks.

One of Paxton's early experiments was an orchid house he built at Chatsworth c. 1836, 'so constructed that scarcely any more light is obstructed than in a metal-roofed house, but it possesses at the same time all the advantages of wood'. Although the roof was made of timber, it was supported with iron columns. It was a sizeable structure, measuring 97½ feet long, 26 feet wide and 15 feet at its highest point. The sashes in the ridge-and-furrow roof were fixed; ventilation was therefore provided by shutters in the back wall and the sliding sashes that formed the front wall. As well as making the wooden glazing bars as narrow as possible, Paxton further increased access to light by introducing grooved glazing bars, so that less putty was needed. Hollow iron columns in the front wall, similar to those made by Jones & Clark at The Grange, acted as downpipes for the rainwater. This building became the prototype for many of his later, better-known designs.

The success of his experiments led to his most ambitious structure to date: the Great Stove. The Duke was an avid collector of exotic plants, having funded several plant-hunting expeditions, even sending some of his young gardeners off around the globe in search of botanical rarities. An additional glasshouse was needed to house these latest exotics, and the Great Stove provided the answer: a vast curvilinear structure with a ridge-and-furrow roof, it covered nearly three-quarters of an acre, measuring 227 feet long, 123 feet wide and 67 feet high at the apex of the roof. Paxton first conceived the idea in 1835, and it was built between 1836 and 1840 for the staggering sum of £33,099 10s 11d, about £1.5 million in today's money. Like the orchid house, it was essentially a timber structure with a ridge-and-furrow roof, but using laminated wooden rafters bent into a curve to create a curvilinear roof. The only iron was in the thirty-six cast-iron columns, which not only supported the roof, but also acted as downpipes for the rainwater draining from the gutters. Because it was built at a time when glass was still taxed, Paxton used the latest techniques in glassmaking: an improved version of the cylinder process that had been developed by the Chance Brothers of Birmingham. This process was able to produce quality glass in much larger sizes, turning out the huge panes that Paxton needed – 48 inches long and 6 inches wide.

Within the Great Stove the tropical and subtropical plants were arranged in a 'Picturesque' style, rather than organised taxonomically as a collection of specimens, an arrangement that was now seen as artificial and unnatural. The plants were placed amongst rockwork and pools of water in order to create a more natural environment, and to give the visitor the impression of a tropical paradise.

The Great Stove became one of the wonders of the age, attracting visitors from all over the land, not least the young Queen Victoria, who was driven down the central aisle in a horse-drawn carriage at night, illuminated by thousands of lamps. Unfortunately the ninth Duke of Devonshire was compelled to have the Stove demolished in the 1920s. The health of the plants had greatly deteriorated during the First World War. The expense of heating such a huge structure (it consumed 300 tons of coal every winter) and the loss of manpower as a result of the war made it a luxury the age could no longer afford. This situation was unfortunately typical of the general decline in such

The magnificent Great Stove at Chatsworth, built between 1836 and 1840 to house the sixth Duke of Devonshire's collection of exotic plants.

buildings at this time. As dismantling the Great Stove was considered too dangerous, it was decided to blow it up, but it was so well built that it took several attempts to do so. All that now remains are the sandstone foundations, evoking the scale of the magnificent building that once stood there.

A surviving example of Paxton's work at Chatsworth is the Conservative Wall, built against a pre-existing hot or forcing wall in the 1840s; the central section was added later, in 1850. This narrow structure, built on a slope, is made up of wooden panels about 27 feet in length, which rise one above the other, an elegant solution to the awkward sloping site. It is about 330 feet long but only 7 feet in width, as its function was to protect the peaches and nectarines trained against the wall.

With the ridge-and-furrow system Paxton demonstrated that a timber structure need not admit any less light than its iron counterpart, thus nullifying one of the chief advantages of iron. However, he was not averse to

The entrance to the Conservative Wall, also known as the Case, at Chatsworth. The central section is planted with camellias.

the material in principle, and he used it extensively in his pair of 90-foot-long lean-to houses at Somerleyton Hall, Suffolk, originally vineries. One is now used as a tearoom, called 'Paxton's Café'.

Paxton's design for the Crystal Palace had its inception as a rough sketch of a ridge-and-furrow structure made on blotting paper during a meeting. Based on his prototypes at Chatsworth, the vast iron and glass building was 135 feet high and covered an area of 773,000 square feet. All its components were prefabricated, making it economical and fast to build: from conception to the opening of the Great Exhibition on 1 May 1851 took just nine months.

Following the triumph of the Crystal Palace, Paxton was knighted, and in 1854 he was elected Member of Parliament for Coventry, a classic example

One of a pair of ridge-and-furrow lean-to vineries at Somerleyton Hall, Suffolk.

Detail showing the ironwork in the ridge-and-furrow roof at Somerleyton Hall.

of the upward mobility possible in the Victorian era. Under the sixth Duke's benevolent patronage Paxton's career had flourished, but, when the Duke died in 1858, Paxton resigned his position of head gardener at Chatsworth. In the same year he turned his attention to a very different kind of project – 'Hothouses for the Million'. Like Loudon before him, Paxton was concerned with broadening the appeal of gardening to include those who could not afford expensive gardening equipment; glasshouses in particular

An advertisement for 'Hothouses for the Million' from the *Gardeners' Chronicle*, 1864.

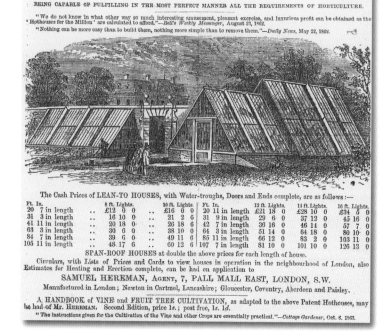

HOTHOUSES FOR THE MILLION.

AWARDED A PRIZE MEDAL, 1862.

ON THE PRINCIPLE INVENTED AND PATENTED BY

SIR JOSEPH PAXTON, M.P.

COMBINING SIMPLICITY, CHEAPNESS, AND DURABILITY.

BEING CAPABLE OF FULFILLING IN THE MOST PERFECT MANNER ALL THE REQUIREMENTS OF HORTICULTURE.

"We do not know in what other way so much interesting amusement, pleasant exercise, and luxurious profit can be obtained as the 'Hothouses for the Million' are calculated to afford."—*Bell's Weekly Messenger*, August 23, 1862.

"Nothing can be more easy than to build them, nothing more simple than to remove them."—*Daily News*, May 22, 1862.

The Cash Prices of LEAN-TO HOUSES, with Water-troughs, Doors and Ends complete, are as follows:—

Ft. In.	8 ft. Lights.		10 ft. Lights.	Ft. In.	12 ft. Lights.	14 ft. Lights.	16 ft. Lights.
20 7 in length	£12 0 0	£16 0 0	20 11 in length	£21 18 0	£28 10 0	£34 5 0
31 3 in length	16 10 0	21 2 6	31 9 in length	29 6 0	37 12 0	45 16 0
41 11 in length	20 18 0	26 18 6	42 7 in length	36 16 0	46 14 0	57 7 0
63 6 in length	30 6 0	38 10 0	64 3 in length	51 14 0	64 18 0	80 10 0
84 7 in length	39 6 0	49 11 6	85 11 in length	66 12 0	83 2 0	103 11 0
105 11 in length	48.17 6	60 12 6	107 7 in length	81 10 0	101 10 0	126 13 0

SPAN-ROOF HOUSES at double the above prices for each length of house.

Circulars, with Lists of Prices and Cards to view houses in operation in the neighbourhood of London, also Estimates for Heating and Erection complete, can be had on application to

SAMUEL HEREMAN, AGENT, 7, PALL MALL EAST, LONDON, S.W.

Manufactured in London; Newton in Cartmel, Lancashire; Gloucester, Coventry, Aberdeen and Paisley.

A HANDBOOK of VINE and FRUIT TREE CULTIVATION, as adapted to the above Patent Hothouses, may be had of Mr. HEREMAN. Second Edition, price 1s.; post free, 1s. 1d.

"The instructions given for the Cultivation of the Vine and other Crops are essentially practical."—*Cottage Gardener*, Oct. 6, 1863.

A 'Paxtonian Plant-house' showing the A-frame structure of one of Paxton's 'Hothouses for the Million', from *The Amateur's Greenhouse and Conservatory*, S. Hibberd, 1883.

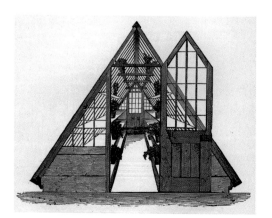

were outside the reach of all but the wealthiest. His idea for portable hothouses was based on a folding hut-frame that he had developed for the British soldiers in the Crimean War. The hothouses were aimed at 'persons having temporary or limited tenure' since they could be simply taken down and moved to a new site when required. Made of timber and glass, they came in a variety of forms, both lean-to and full-span, the tops hinged to form a tent-like structure. They were available in a range of sizes, from 20 to 100 feet in length, costing from £12 for the smallest to about £150 for the largest. His former secretary, Samuel Hereman, acted as agent for their manufacture and sale.

A Paxtonian house adapted for growing cucumbers, 1883.

Whilst the ridge and furrow system had its moment of glory, its influence was limited to comparatively few examples, mostly built by Paxton, possibly because of the added expense (almost twice as much glass was needed for the roofs). But he had made a convincing case for the use of timber structures, and, as the fashion for iron-framed glasshouses waned, so the appeal of wooden glasshouses grew. Paxton's concern for the humble amateur came at a time when manufacturers were more preoccupied with their wealthier clientele, and thus he encouraged others to provide more economically priced versions for this particular market.

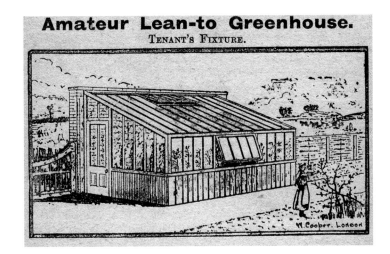

Manufacturers such as William Cooper Ltd offered economical lean-to structures suitable for amateurs and tenants.

MESSENGER & CO.LTD.

LOUGHBOROUGH
AND LONDON

HORTICULTURAL SECTION
FIFTH EDITION

THE MASS-PRODUCED GLASSHOUSE

In the popular mind nothing so accurately indicates the extent of a man's wealth, in the absence of first-hand information on the point, as the quantity of glass which adorns his mansion and grounds; and a tolerably good guide it is too.

The Northern Echo, 1889.

FROM THE MIDDLE of the nineteenth century, breakthroughs in heating and glazing led to a dramatic growth in the number of manufacturers specialising in 'horticultural buildings'. Glasshouses were now within the reach of the burgeoning middle classes, and their manufacture created a new and lucrative market that was met by firms offering prefabricated glasshouses to suit every need. Timber-framed houses became increasingly popular, particularly in productive gardens, being not only better insulated than iron, but also more economical to mass-produce. This market became highly competitive, with most manufacturers offering a package that included heating apparatus, interior staging and other optional extras.

Developments in heating and glazing were the two key drivers in the mass-production of glasshouses. The old inefficient hot-air flue system of the eighteenth century was now outdated. At the turn of the century it was briefly superseded by steam heating, whereby water was heated and condensed in boilers before being driven through perforated pipes set in gravel beneath the plant beds. This system, though cleaner and in many ways more efficient than the old, was still fraught with problems: it could cause excessive condensation; it needed constant attention; and there were occasionally terrible accidents with exploding boilers. Various inventions for heating with hot water were pioneered in the early decades of the nineteenth century, and, by the 1840s, these had been sufficiently perfected to become the heating method of choice. Water was heated in large coal-fired boilers and circulated around the glasshouses in 6-inch cast-iron pipes, which were placed beneath the staging and under the pathway gratings. This method

Opposite:
The cover of the Messenger catalogue, c. 1900, shows an elaborate conservatory with decorative stained glass, clearly intended to be used as an 'outdoor room'.

An advertisement in the horticultural press in 1862 for J. Weeks and Company of London, showing an elaborate range of glasshouses with a brief list of some of their most eminent clients. The 'urns' on the wall are most likely chimneys in disguise.

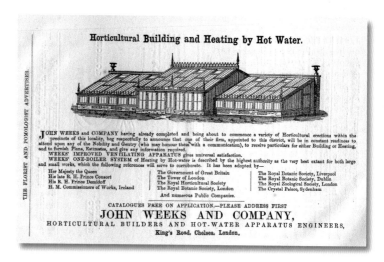

was not only less labour-intensive, but also more reliable and economical, although the huge boilers could devour massive amounts of coal.

The Chance Brothers of the West Midlands had already introduced their improved method of making cylinder glass sheet when, in 1845, Robert Peel's government repealed the glass tax. The resulting fall in the price of glass was dramatic; it directly benefited the glass trade, thereby boosting the demand for glasshouses. The availability of larger panes of glass now enabled the glazing bars to be spaced further apart (about 12 inches), so admitting more light into the house. As in earlier structures, the panes were overlapped and puttied in. The use of scalloped 'fish-tail' or 'beaver-tail' glass, known as 'circular' glass earlier in the century, now became the norm, the idea being to channel the rainwater away from the glazing bars, thereby avoiding moisture ingress under the putty and into the wood.

Now that glazing and heating were cheaper, manufacturers could offer a wider choice of structures: full-span and three-quarter span as well as lean-to

The range of 'Robin Hood' hot-water boilers made by the Beeston Foundry Company, a subsidiary of Foster & Pearson Ltd.

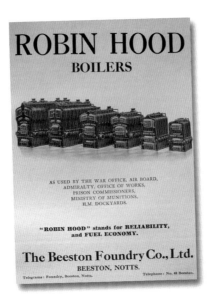

Opposite:
A range of the different span houses offered by Mackenzie & Moncur Ltd; from their 1900 catalogue.

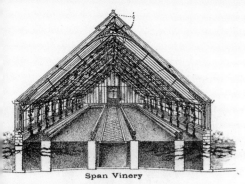

Span Vinery

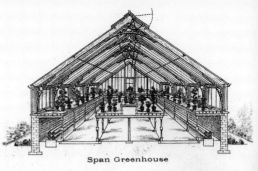

Span Greenhouse

Three-quarter-span Vinery

Three-quarter-span Greenhouse

Lean-to Greenhouse

Lean-to Vinery

Conservatory with Straight Roof

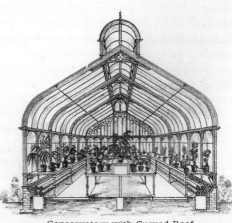

Conservatory with Curved Roof

houses became available. Three-quarter and full-span houses provided more space and light; the former were placed against a wall, in the manner of a lean-to, but could achieve a greater height since the apex of the glasshouse exceeded the height of the wall. Full-span glasshouses could be sited anywhere so long as they were placed on a north-south axis. They were sometimes constructed immediately outside a walled garden so as not to take up valuable growing space. The lean-to was the cheapest and commonest type of house used for fruit-growing, but a high south-facing wall, against which it was built, was essential.

Also available was a range of different houses tailored for specific crops. For fruit there were vineries, fig houses and peach houses; a cheaper option for the latter was a 'peach case', a narrow lean-to structure where peaches were trained against the wall. Special houses were made for flowering plants such as orchids, chrysanthemums, heaths and auriculas.

Most manufacturers constructed houses in both iron and timber, but many stressed the superiority of timber, particularly in relation to conductivity, and advised their clients accordingly. One firm gave the ratios of conductivity as: iron 450, deal 3. The commonest timber used was Baltic pine, also known as 'red deal' or 'pitch pine', a slow-growing softwood from Sweden, Norway and Russia, which was of superior strength and durability. The wood was generally painted with lead paint and needed frequent repainting, at least every three or four years. An alternative was teak, a hard wood from Burma, specially recommended for houses with high humidity such as orchid houses. Teak did not require painting and was therefore cheaper to maintain, although it was much more expensive to buy initially. Whilst the main material was timber, in the more expensive houses iron was used throughout to reinforce the structure.

Manufacturers developed their own 'house styles', using their ironwork to display their own

A span-roofed orchid house by Boulton & Paul Ltd of Norwich. The plants were grown in pots placed on staging; the central staging is placed over a water tank to increase the humidity of the house.

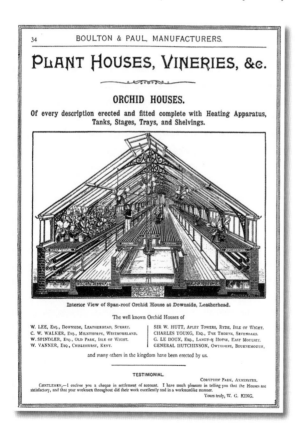

34   BOULTON & PAUL, MANUFACTURERS.

PLANT HOUSES, VINERIES, &c.

ORCHID HOUSES.

Of every description erected and fitted complete with Heating Apparatus, Tanks, Stages, Trays, and Shelvings.

Interior View of Span-roof Orchid House at Downside, Leatherhead.

The well known Orchid Houses of

W. LEE, Esq., DOWNSIDE, LEATHERHEAD, SURREY.
C. W. WALKER, Esq., MILNTHORPE, WESTMORELAND.
W. SPINDLER, Esq., OLD PARK, ISLE OF WIGHT.
W. VANNER, Esq., CHISLEHURST, KENT.

SIR W. HUTT, APLEY TOWERS, RYDE, ISLE OF WIGHT.
CHARLES YOUNG, Esq., THE THORNS, SEVENOAKS.
G. LE DOUX, Esq., LANGTON HOUSE, EAST MOULSEY.
GENERAL HUTCHINSON, OWTHORPE, BOURNEMOUTH.

and many others in the kingdom have been erected by us.

TESTIMONIAL.

CORYPTON PARK, AXMINSTER.

GENTLEMEN,—I enclose you a cheque in settlement of account. I have much pleasure in telling you that the Houses are satisfactory, and that your workmen throughout did their work excellently and in a workmanlike manner.

Yours truly, W. G. KING.

distinctive, and often elaborate, decorations, with elegantly crafted spandrels, ridge crestings, finials and floor gratings available in a range of patterns. The more functional ironwork, such as the ventilation mechanisms, was often stamped with the maker's name.

Manufacturers issued illustrated catalogues describing their products and usually included lists of their clients, enabling them to boast of their noble, and often royal, patrons (who were always listed first). Each manufacturer attempted to position itself in the market by offering a unique selling point, from 'cheap houses for amateurs or nurseries' to 'conservatories of the most chaste and elegant designs'.

One of the earliest and most successful of these was Foster & Pearson Ltd, established in 1841 in Beeston, Nottingham. It was a partnership between the Pearson family, a long-established firm of nurserymen from Chilwell, Nottinghamshire, and Richard Foster, a joiner from nearby Beeston. A subsidiary company, the Beeston Foundry Company (later known as the Beeston Boiler Company Ltd), was established in 1888 by Henry and Louis Pearson, in order to manufacture cast-iron boilers for heating the glasshouses. Their range included the famous 'Robin Hood' boiler, so called because of the proximity of Sherwood Forest. Foster & Pearson became one of the leading glasshouse manufacturers in Britain, with an extensive range of clients, from Queen Victoria to the famous Veitch Nurseries in Chelsea.

As one of the earliest of the glasshouse manufacturers, Foster & Pearson claimed to lead the way in innovative methods of construction and ventilation. In order to admit as much light as possible, they cut down on the amount of timber used in the frame by supporting the structure with cast-iron columns. Decorative cast-iron 'muntins', or mullions, were used between the casements for supporting the front of the roof. A vaunted feature was their 'improved

Above Left:
Decorative finials available in a range of styles, from the Mackenzie & Moncur catalogue, 1900. The thistle design on no. 2 is a recurring motif of the Scottish firm.

Above:
A quadrant lever for operating the front casements, stamped with the maker's name: 'Messenger & Co'.

47

Selection from List of Clients.

Names of a few, out of many thousands, of the Nobility and Gentry throughout England, and in Wales, Scotland, Ireland, the Isle of Man, the Channel Islands, and Abroad, for whom we have executed orders.

UNDER THE DISTINGUISHED PATRONAGE OF

HER MOST GRACIOUS MAJESTY THE LATE QUEEN VICTORIA.

HIS ROYAL HIGHNESS THE LATE PRINCE CONSORT.

His Majesty's Board of Works.

The Royal Horticultural Society.

Her Imperial Majesty The Empress Eugenie.
His Highness Prince Louis of Hesse.
His Highness The late Prince Demidoff.
His Highness The late Viceroy of Egypt.
His Grace The Lord Archbishop of Canterbury.

His Grace The Duke of Beaufort.
His Grace The Duke of Bedford.
His Grace The Duke of Devonshire.
His Grace The Duke of Fife.
His Grace The Duke of Leeds.
His Grace The Duke of Marlborough.
His Grace The Duke of Norfolk.
His Grace The Duke of Northumberland.
His Grace The Duke of Portland.
His Grace The Duke of Richmond.
His Grace The Duke of Rutland.
His Grace The Duke of Roxburghe.
His Grace The Duke of Somerset.
His Grace The Duke of Sutherland.
His Grace The Duke of Westminster.

The Most Honorable The Marquis of Aylesbury.
The Most Honorable The Marquis of Bute.
The Most Honorable The Marquis of Bath.
The Most Honorable The Marquis of Blandford.

The Most Honorable The Marquis of Bredalbane.
The Most Honorable The Marquis of Camden.
The Most Honorable The Marquis of Downshire.
The Most Honorable The Marquis of Drogheda.
The Most Honorable The Marquis of Exeter.
The Most Honorable The Marquis of Townsend.
The Most Honorable The Marquis of Waterford.
The Most Honorable The Marquis of Winchester.
The Marquis Corsi di Salviati.
The Dowager Marchioness of Bath.
The Marchioness of Downshire.
The Marchioness De Castegu.
The Baron Diegadt.
The Baron Bruno Schröder.
The Baron F. de Rothschild.
The Baron Profumo.
The Baroness Gray.
The Baroness Burdett Coutts.
The Baroness Dimsdale.
The Dowager Countess Cowper.
The Countess of Bridgewater.
The Countess of Arlie.
The Countess of Winchelsea.

The Right Honorable The Earl of Aylesford.
The Right Honorable The Earl of Amherst.

The Right Honorable The Earl of Ashbroke.
The Right Honorable The Earl of Ancaster.
The Right Honorable The Earl of Bective.
The Right Honorable The Earl of Bridport.
The Right Honorable The Earl of Beauchamp.
The Right Honorable The Earl of Bessborough.
The Right Honorable The Earl of Crawford.
The Right Honorable The Earl of Courtown.
The Right Honorable The Earl of Cottenham.
The Right Honorable The Earl of Coventry.
The Right Honorable The Earl of Carysfort.
The Right Honorable The Earl of Crewe.
The Right Honorable The Earl De la Warr.
The Right Honorable The Earl of Dysart.
The Right Honorable The Earl of Derby.
The Right Honorable The Earl of Ellesmere.
The Right Honorable The Earl of Essex.
The Right Honorable The Earl of Fortescue.
The Right Honorable The Earl of Harrowby.
The Right Honorable The Earl of Hardwicke.
The Right Honorable The Earl of Jersey.
The Right Honorable The Earl of Kilmorey.
The Right Honorable The Earl of Kenmare.
The Right Honorable The Earl of Leicester.
The Right Honorable The Earl of Lisburne.

The first page of the list of clients from J. Weeks & Company's catalogue, listing the most illustrious first.

A brass Foster & Pearson door latch, stamped with the manufacturer's name.

glazing bar', which had grooves cut into the underside of the bar, designed to catch any drips of water from condensation and prevent them falling on the plants. Another was a unique form of ventilation: the vertical rising ridge ventilation system, whereby a lantern running along the entire length of the roof could be raised to release the hot air, a method later adopted by some other firms.

The glasshouses of the preceding century had sliding roof sashes for ventilation, which had to be opened individually, as did the front casements. The system adopted by nearly all the nineteenth-century manufacturers was the 'universal system', whereby the upper lights could be raised and lowered in a butterfly movement in one operation. This was achieved by means of a long rod, connected to the opening lights with elbow levers; the rod could then be made to rotate by a winding mechanism, usually located on the back wall, thus causing the lights to open or close. The front lights were operated in much the same way, but generally with a lever or winch.

Thomas Goode Messenger had established a plumbing and glazing business in Loughborough High Street, Leicestershire, and went on to form Messenger & Company Ltd in 1858, producing horticultural buildings. Ten years later, the success of the company was such that

The rising ridge ventilator in a Foster & Pearson span house.

larger premises, including an iron foundry, were established at the edge of the town, taking advantage of the adjacent railway by having its own siding. The firm soon became one of the premier glasshouse manufacturers in the country, with a broad client base. Like Foster & Pearson, Messenger aimed to reduce the dimensions of the timber in order to admit more light, but they used a different method in that they reinforced the frame with iron tension rods. For houses with high condensation such as orchid houses, they also offered a specially grooved glazing bar to prevent dripping on the plants beneath, very similar to that of Foster & Pearson.

An advertisement for Messenger & Company's 'modern glasshouses' in the *Gardener's Magazine*, 1913, includes an unsolicited testimonial.

The development of the railways from the 1840s was crucial to the rise in mass-produced glasshouses, since it made possible long-distance delivery of the prefabricated parts to all corners of Britain, which could then be erected on site either by the estate staff or by the manufacturer's own team. Another firm well-positioned to exploit the rail system was W. Richardson & Company of Darlington, whose factory had its own siding on the main Edinburgh-London railway line. William Richardson was a Quaker with an architectural background; his first venture, the North of England Horticultural Works, was established in 1874 and later became known as W. Richardson & Company. The firm specialised in timber glasshouses using Baltic pine, and, whilst iron-framed houses could be made on request, the catalogue warned that 'we cannot recommend them'. Their main innovation seems to have been a curious method of ventilation (see page 3 illustration), whereby a glazed frame 13 inches wide, and the entire height of the roof from top to bottom, could be raised by means of levers. Bottom ventilation was achieved by wooden shutters built into the front wall that could be opened simultaneously with a single lever handle. It is not apparent what the advantages were of this 'patent system', nor how popular it proved with their clients.

The Scottish firm Mackenzie & Moncur Ltd was founded by two joiners, Alexander Mackenzie and George Moncur, who met in Edinburgh and formed a partnership in 1869 in order to build timber glasshouses; a foundry was a later addition so that iron-framed structures could also be offered. By the end of the century they had established a reputation for building elaborate ranges of outstanding quality. From their branches in Glasgow, Edinburgh and London they supplied clients throughout Britain and indeed the world, clients who included members of the royal family, notably Queen Victoria and the Prince of Wales. They boasted of using only the best-quality St Petersburg redwood or teak.

There was an attempt to revive curvilinear metal-framed glasshouses in the late nineteenth century. Vincent Skinner had set up a business manufacturing heating apparatus in Bristol in 1858. He later formed a partnership with Henry Board, and so Skinner, Board & Company was founded in 1884. They developed a new method of glazing a glasshouse without the use of putty, which they patented as their 'wire tension'

A page from the Mackenzie & Moncur catalogue, 1900, itemising their products.

greenhouse. The houses were constructed with curved iron rafters about 2 to 3 feet apart; galvanised steel rods were threaded through them from one end of the house to the other, the height of a pane of glass apart. Sprung steel clips were attached to the rods, and the glass was inserted into the clips, which thus held it in place, each pane overlapping the one beneath, producing a curvilinear structure with little obstruction of light. They had the added advantage of not requiring painting, and were therefore more economical

An advertisement for Skinner, Board & Company's 'wire tension greenhouses'.

to maintain than timber houses. Such structures were versatile: they could be adapted to any span and built in a range of sizes. They were also supplied with flat roofs.

Towards the end of the nineteenth century, many of these firms concentrated on the heating installation side of their business, to meet the growing demand for domestic, as well as glasshouse, heating. The First World War impacted not only on the manufacturers, but also, perhaps more significantly, on their clients, for many of the landowning class, and of their gardening staff, had been killed in the war. The demand for glasshouses and conservatories declined dramatically. There was neither the manpower nor the money for the upkeep of extensive ranges of glass, and when glasshouses became derelict they were not replaced.

Most manufacturers struggled on well into the twentieth century, attempting, in spite of the Second World War, to adapt to new technologies and markets. Messenger & Company, having moved into the heating trade, closed down in 1980. Their derelict works still remains in Loughborough. Richardson & Company went into receivership in 1980, when they were taken on by Amdega, who continued to make conservatories and glasshouses until 2011, when they were bought by Everest. Skinner, Board & Company Ltd continued to trade throughout the twentieth century as air-conditioning engineers and plumbers. Mackenzie & Moncur split into several subsidiary companies, the last of which ceased trading in 1998.

A postcard, 1911, showing a splendid range of Skinner, Board & Company glasshouses in the walled garden at Pell Wall, Market Drayton, Shropshire. Their condition suggests they were recently erected.

RESTORATION

When considering the restoration of a glasshouse or conservatory, it is important to keep in mind its functional use and future maintenance requirements. Most structures have declined after years of little maintenance: unpainted glazing bars, unreplaced broken glass and uncleared gutters will have resulted in serious water ingress ... resulting in rot and rust.

John Watkins and Tom Wright (editors), *The Management and Maintenance of Historic Parks, Gardens and Landscapes* (2007).

THE MAJORITY OF EARLY GLASSHOUSES were abandoned around the middle of the twentieth century, when they became no longer viable financially. They were left to deteriorate and decay, or were demolished and removed. Happily, a significant number have been saved from dereliction and have been carefully restored to their original condition. Glasshouse restoration can be extremely expensive: funding is available, but it tends to favour structures of historic interest situated in gardens open to the public, whilst private owners are often left to foot the bill themselves. However, throughout the United Kingdom there are many excellent examples of restorations to be found, mostly of glasshouses dating from the nineteenth and early twentieth centuries.

Iron-framed glasshouses survive better, and there are several restored examples that can be visited by the public. The vinery at Arundel Castle, West Sussex, was restored in the late 1990s by Carden & Godfrey Architects. It was built by Clark & Hope for the thirteenth Duke of Norfolk in 1853, along with a peach house that has since been demolished. The vinery is an iron-framed lean-to structure 100 feet long and 15 feet wide, with the copper glazing bars typical of this firm, as are the Gothic-style iron doors. Some of the ironwork had to be replaced, but much of it was sound, merely requiring shot-blasting to remove the dirt and rust before reinstatement. About 80 per cent of the original scalloped glass was removed and cleaned, and supplemented with new UMV glass, which is a blown glass visually

Opposite:
Aerial view
of some of
the sixteen
fully restored
and working
glasshouses
at West Dean
Gardens, West
Sussex.

Above:
The winding mechanism for operating the sliding roof sashes, stamped with the maker's name, in the vinery at Arundel Castle.

Above right:
The Clark & Hope iron-framed vinery at Arundel Castle, West Sussex. Originally built in 1853, it was restored in 1996–7.

compatible with the nineteenth-century glass. This was mixed in at random, thereby disguising any discrepancy between the old and new panes. There are sliding roof sashes for ventilation, worked in the manner typical of these early glasshouses, by a pulley system with a winding ratchet for each sash on the back walls. The old hot-water boiler system was removed and the house is now heated with a modern gas boiler.

The fernery at Ascog Hall, on the Isle of Bute, was built in the 1870s, when the craze for collecting ferns, or 'pteridomania', was at its peak. Not only was the British countryside scoured for native ferns that could be grown outside, but more exotic species could be obtained from nurseries such as Loddiges, Veitch & Sons and Backhouse & Son. These more tender varieties need some kind of protection under glass; an ordinary plant house or conservatory might be adapted for this purpose, but for the serious collector, a special house, or fernery, was required. The Ascog fernery is an excellent Victorian example, within which an elaborate 'landscape' of rocks, water and ferns was created in imitation of the plants' natural habitat. It was restored by the owners in the 1990s, and beautifully replanted with many of the original species based on a description in the *Gardener's Chronicle* in 1879, assisted by the Royal Botanic Gardens, Edinburgh.

It is an L-shaped structure with rounded ends, sunk into the earth, so that the iron-framed span-roof, resting upon stone walls, is at ground level. This subterranean design protects against heat loss, allowing tender and subtropical plants to be grown without additional heat. The visitor descends some stone steps to enter a verdant scene of tall tree-ferns, moss-covered

An engraving showing the interior of the fernery at Ascog Hall, Bute, in the *Gardener's Chronicle*, 1879.

rocks and a central pool fed by a small waterfall. Because of the wet and humid atmosphere, the structure had to be constructed in iron, which in part explains its remarkable survival.

The interior of the fernery at Ascog before restoration, early 1990s.

The interior of the Ascog fernery after restoration, photographed in 2010.

Timber glasshouses can deteriorate rapidly when they are no longer maintained; it is perhaps surprising that a wooden structure can survive for as long as one hundred years or more: that it can do so is evidence of the quality of the timber then most commonly used. This was the slow-growing Baltic redwood, or pitch pine, which is superior to much of the timber on sale today, but North American Douglas fir has similar qualities and is readily available, and is therefore the timber of choice for most restoration projects. Teak is another option, initially more expensive to buy, but more economical to maintain.

Timber houses built before the First World War were painted with lead paint, which probably offers the best protection for wooden structures, but is now banned because of its toxicity. However, for some historic structures a licence to use it may be obtained. There are several modern alternatives, such as micro-porous and linseed paints. In a historically significant structure, hand-made glass is most likely to be used, particularly if it is situated in a heritage property open to the public, but, for private owners, ordinary horticultural glass can suffice.

West Dean Gardens in West Sussex have a magnificent collection of fully stocked and working timber glasshouses, sixteen in all, built by Foster & Pearson at the end of the nineteenth century. All types are represented: lean-tos, full-spans, cold-frames and pit-houses, within which a wide range of plants is grown, including orchids, figs, nectarines, peaches and grapes. The restoration of the glasshouses, which were very derelict, took place between 1992 and 1994. They are now lovingly maintained with a thorough annual cleaning, both inside and out, and are repainted on a rolling cycle about every four years, the exteriors in summer and the interiors in winter.

The Citrus House at Margam Country Park in South Wales, listed grade II*, is an unusual structure: not an orangery as the name suggests, but a long, narrow lean-to glasshouse, where the trees were once trained on

Photographs taken before and after restoration (1992–3) of one of the ranges at West Dean Gardens. The range is made up of two vineries and a fig house. The fig house is the one visible at the end.

trellis against the back wall, in the manner of a peach case; indeed, it was originally referred to as the 'Orange Wall'. Having become derelict, the structure has been restored as the late-nineteenth-century replacement for the original, which was built in 1800. The central, undivided glazed section, approximately 126 feet long, lies between two pavilions at either end. It has

a double pitched roof, supported centrally with a row of iron columns, with a narrow bed running along the front. In the past the lights, most likely the lower roof lights, were removed in May and replaced in October. In 1842 it was described as housing forty trees. Restoration by Acanthus Holden Architects began in 2010 and the house was reopened in 2012. Douglas fir was used throughout. The ironwork was shot-blasted and repaired where necessary, and toughened scalloped panes of glass were used, in keeping with the originals.

Photographs taken before (2009: top) and after (2012: right) the restoration of the citrus house at Margam Park, South Wales.

The timber lean-to range in the walled garden at Audley End, Essex, was originally built in 1803 to replace an orangery, making it an unusually early survival. It has the features one would expect of a house of this date, such as sliding roof sashes counterbalanced with lead weights, and the front sashes slide sideways. The range comprises a central show house, with a vinery and a peach house on either side. The range to the left of the show house was heated for early crops, and that on the right unheated. It was restored by English Heritage in the second half of the 1990s, and is a fine example of

The interior of the citrus house at Margam Park, nearing completion.

The refurbished range at Audley End, Essex (2012). The range was fully restored in the 1990s. In the second section the vines can be seen planted outside, the rods trained through holes in the front wall.

Interior of one of the vineries at Audley End, with the vines trained up under the roof. The lead weights for counter-balancing the roof sashes can be seen hanging against the back wall.

a Georgian glasshouse, originally built by estate staff, before prefabricated structures became available.

When glasshouses are beyond repair or have been removed, they can be reconstructed by closely following what remains of the original structure and by reusing what materials can be salvaged.

At Tatton Park, a National Trust property run by Cheshire Council, restoration of the walled garden began in 1995. A very large Georgian glasshouse, then thought to be a vinery, had, until its loss in 1959, been the centrepiece of the productive garden. Its recovery followed a programme of detailed research in 2002 that demonstrated that a 120-foot-long building, first proposed by Samuel Wyatt in 1776, had been constructed in three compartments against a heated wall. Within each of the compartments was a deep brick-built bed, which would have been originally filled with fermenting tan bark or oak leaves in which pineapples were grown. The glasshouse served as a vinery too, for archaeological excavation demonstrated that the front wall had a deeply prepared and well-drained border on the outside, in which the vines were planted, with perforations in the front wall through which their stems were drawn inside.

The reconstruction closely followed the evidence of the original, including the use of 6-inch hand-made glass. The timber, western red cedar, is painted with linseed oil paint. The sliding roof sashes, counterbalanced with lead weights, provide ventilation. In 2012 pineapples were grown and ripened successfully for the first time, the pits being filled with oak leaves rather than tan bark. This glasshouse is now the only full-scale working Georgian pinery-vinery in the United Kingdom.

Croome Court is also a National Trust property, but the major part of the walled kitchen garden is privately owned. This includes a range of

The reconstructed eighteenth-century pinery-vinery at Tatton Park, Cheshire, completed in 2007.

glasshouses, comprising a melon house, a fig house and a vinery, all of which have been gradually restored over the years by the owners. Although no fig was present, the fig house is so called since it was described as such in an article in the *Gardening World* in 1887. The present house has been reconstructed as an exact replica of the original, which was probably built by estate staff in the early nineteenth century.

A span plant house, originally built by Boulton & Paul Ltd, a nineteenth-century manufacturer based in Norwich, had to be completely reconstructed by the Victorian Glasshouse Company, as the timber was too badly decayed to be reused. The mouldings of the original timber were copied in iroko,

The interior of the pinery-vinery at Tatton Park, showing pineapples planted in pots, placed in a bed filled with oak leaves.

The fig house at Croome Court, Worcestershire, completely rebuilt by the owners. It now houses a fig, trained up the back wall, and other tender plants such as olives and citrus.

a hard wood with similar properties to teak in that it does not need painting, but which is less expensive. The original ironwork was blast-treated and galvanised in dark grey.

Such restored and productive houses are a testament to the quality of the original designs, and they continue their productive role today, albeit with improvements such as modern heating methods and toughened glass. However, restoration is only the first stage of a glasshouse's second life, and continued maintenance is essential if it is to last another hundred years or more.

A Boulton & Paul span house in the process of reconstruction, using iroko hardwood. It was later glazed with 3 mm horticultural glass.

LIST OF MANUFACTURERS

Bailey, W. & D., Holborn, London; established 1818. Later D. & E. Bailey; from *c.* 1830s.

Boulton & Paul Ltd, Norwich, Norfolk; established 1864.

Cooper, William, Old Kent Road, London; *c.* 1893.

Cottam & Hallen, Oxford Street, London; established by 1840s.

Crompton & Fawkes, Chelmsford, Essex; trading 1880s.

Fletcher, Lowndes & Company, St George Street, London; trading 1870s.

Foster & Pearson Ltd, Beeston, Nottinghamshire; established 1841.

Halliday, R., & Company, Middleton, Manchester; trading 1880s.

Hope, Henry, Lionel Street, Birmingham; from 1875.

Jones & Clark, Birmingham; established 1818, later Clark & Hope, 1864.

Macfarlane, Walter, & Company, Glasgow; trading 1870s.

Mackenzie & Moncur Ltd, Edinburgh; established 1869.

Cross-section of a peach house by Weeks & Company, 1879.

Fig. 47.—WEEKS'S PEACH HOUSE.

Messenger & Company, Loughborough, Leicestershire; established 1858.
Ormson, Henry, Kings Road, London; established 1870s (previously
 Gray & Ormson).
Rendle, William Edgcumbe, Plymouth; trading 1870s.
Richardson, W., & Company, Darlington, Co. Durham; trading 1870s.
Skinner, Board & Company, Rupert Street, Bristol; established c. 1887.
Strawson, G. F., & Son, Horley, Surrey; established c. 1892.
Tucker, Duncan, Tottenham, London; established 1830.
Turner, Richard, Hammersmith, Dublin; trading 1830s.
Weeks, J., & Company, Kings Road, London; established c. 1836.
Wrinch & Sons, Ipswich and London; trading 1890s.

PLACES TO VISIT

Arundel Castle, Arundel, West Sussex BN18 9AB.
 Telephone: 01903 882173.
 Website: www.arundelcastle.org/_pages/02_gardens.htm
Ascog Hall, Ascog, Isle of Bute, Scotland PA20 9EU.
 Telephone: 01700 504555.
 Website: www.ascoghallfernery.co.uk
 Unusual sunken fernery, fully restored and planted.
Attingham Park, Atcham, Shrewsbury, Shropshire SY4 4TP.
 Telephone: 01743 708162.
 Website: www.nationaltrust.org.uk/attingham-park
 Restored early-twentieth-century Duncan Tucker glasshouses: a range
 of lean-tos and a span melon house, all in use.
Audley End, Saffron Walden, Essex CB11 4JF. Telephone: 01799 522842.
 Website: www.english heritage.org.uk/daysout/properties/
 audley-end-house-and-garden
 Restored early-nineteenth-century range comprising vineries,
 peach houses and show house. There is also an unusual orchard
 house originally built by the fruit horticulturalist Thomas Rivers.
Bicton Botanic Gardens, East Budleigh, Budleigh Salterton, Devon EX9 7BJ.
 Telephone: 01395 568465.
 Website: www.bictongardens.co.uk
 Magnificent early Victorian palm house by the Baileys;
 also a tropical house.
Calke Abbey, Ticknall, Derby DE73 7LE. Telephone: 01332 863822.
 National Trust.
 Website: www.nationaltrust.org.uk/calke-abbey
 Eighteenth-century glass-domed orangery; also productive glasshouses
 in the walled garden.

Chatsworth House, Bakewell, Derbyshire DE45 1PP.
Telephone: 01246 565300. Website: www.chatsworth.org
As well as Paxton's well-known Conservative Wall or Case, there are
also working glasshouses by Foster & Pearson and Messenger.

Clumber Park, Worksop, Nottinghamshire S80 3AZ.
Telephone: 01909 476592. National Trust.
Website: www.nationaltrust.org.uk/clumber-park
Impressive range of glass 250 feet long, made up of twelve distinct
glasshouses, including a central conservatory and palm house, all in
full production.

Copped Hall Walled Kitchen Garden, Copped Hall, Crown Hill, Epping,
Essex CM16 5HS. Telephone: 01992 571657.
Website: www.coppedhalltrust.org.uk
There are ten Victorian glasshouses, gradually being restored by
the Copped Hall Trust.

Cragside, Rothbury, Northumberland NE65 7PX.
Telephone: 01669 620333. National Trust.
Website: www.nationaltrust.org.uk/cragside
Range of glasshouses includes an orchard house with revolving stands
for fruit-trees in pots, restored and planted.

Croome Court Walled Gardens, Gardeners Cottage, Croome, Severn Stoke,
Worcestershire WR8 9DW. Website: www.croomewalledgardens.com
Privately owned walled garden with restored glasshouses. Open by
appointment; contact via the website.

Helmsley Walled Garden, Cleveland Way, Helmsley, North Yorkshire YO62 5AH.
Telephone: 01439 771427.
Website: www.helmsleywalledgarden.org.uk
Various restored glasshouses including a display house and vineries,
one of which houses the café.

Holkham Hall, Wells-next-the-Sea, Norfolk NR23 1AB.
Telephone: 01328 710227.
Website: www.holkham.co.uk/html/walledgardens.html
Numerous late-nineteenth-century glasshouses, comprising a large
range of restored vineries, pit houses and frames.

The Lost Gardens of Heligan, Pentewan, St Austell, Cornwall PL26 6EN.
Telephone: 01726 845100. Website: www.heligan.com
Restored glasshouses include a pineapple pit, a lean-to vinery,
peach house and citrus house.

Luton Hoo Walled Garden, Luton Hoo, Luton, Bedfordshire LU1 4LF.
Telephone: 01582 879089. Website: www.lutonhoowalledgarden.org.uk
Magnificent range of Mackenzie & Moncur glasshouses, awaiting
restoration.

Margam Country Park, Port Talbot, South Wales SA13 2AG.
Telephone: 01639 881635. Website: www.margamcountrypark.co.uk
Impressive eighteenth-century orangery and unusual restored
citrus house.

Mertoun Gardens, St Boswells, Melrose, Roxburghshire TD6 0EA.
Telephone: 01835 823236. Website: www.mertoungardens.com
Skinner, Board & Company glasshouses, containing perfectly trained
figs and peaches.

Osborne House, East Cowes, Isle of Wight PO32 6JX.
Telephone: 01983 200022. English Heritage. Website:
www.english-heritage.org.uk/daysout/properties/osborne-house
Restored 1850s Clark & Hope vinery.

Somerleyton Hall, Lowestoft, Suffolk NR32 5QQ.
Telephone: 01502 734901.
Website: www.somerleyton.co.uk/hallgardens
Paxton peach cases and ridge and furrow vineries.

Syon House, Syon Park, Brentford, Middlesex TW8 8JF.
Telephone: 0208 569 7497. Website: www.syonpark.co.uk
Spectacular conservatory with domed roof built in metal and
Bath stone by Charles Fowler in 1826.

Tatton Park, Knutsford, Cheshire WA16 6QN.
Telephone: 01625 374400. Website: www.tattonpark.org.uk
The restored eighteenth-century pinery-vinery by Samuel Wyatt
produced its first crop of pineapples in 2012. There is also an
impressive fernery, an orangery and a range of working glasshouses.

The Walled Nursery, Water Lane, Hawkhurst, Kent TN18 5DH.
Telephone: 01580 752752. Website: www.thewallednursery.com
Thirteen Foster & Pearson glasshouses, including a melon house,
vinery, fernery and peach house.

West Dean Gardens, West Dean, Chichester, West Sussex PO18 0QZ.
Telephone: 01243 818210.
Website: www.westdean.org.uk/Garden/Home.aspx
Superb range of sixteen fully stocked working glasshouses by Foster &
Pearson: vineries, peach, melon and orchid houses.

BOTANIC GARDENS

Belfast Botanic Gardens, College Park, Botanic Avenue, Belfast BT7 1LP.
Telephone: 0289 031 4762 or 07767 271683.
Website: www.belfastcity.gov.uk/parksandopenspaces/ palmhouse.asp
The curvilinear iron and glass structure is the first work of ironmaster
Richard Turner, begun in 1839, designed by the architect Charles
Lanyon. The central section was added later.

Birmingham Botanical Gardens, Westbourne Road, Edgbaston, Birmingham
B15 3TR. Telephone: 0121 454 1660.
Website: www.birminghambotanicalgardens.org.uk
There are four glasshouses, the earliest by Clark & Hope and later
Henry Hope: tropical (1851), palm (1871), Mediterranean and
arid houses (both 1873).

Glasgow Botanic Gardens, 730 Great Western Road, Glasgow G12 0UE.
Telephone: 0141 276 1614.
Website: www.glasgow.gov.uk/en/residents/parks_outdoors/
parks_gardens/botanicgardens.htm
Home of the Kibble Palace, a magnificent late Victorian curvilinear iron
and glass structure, now fully restored.

National Botanic Gardens, Glasnevin, Dublin.
Telephone: 353 1 804 0300. Website: www.botanicgardens.ie
Superb curvilinear range of glasshouses by Richard Turner, fully restored.

Royal Botanic Garden Edinburgh, 20A Inverleith Row, Edinburgh EH3 5LR.
Telephone: 0131 552 7171.
Website: www.rbge.org.uk/the-gardens/edinburgh/the-glasshouses
The Tropical and Temperate Palm Houses are substantial structures,
built of sandstone, iron and glass in 1834 and 1858 respectively.

The Royal Botanic Gardens, Kew, Richmond, Surrey TW9 3AB.
Telephone: 01444 894066.
Website: www.kew.org/visit-kew-gardens/garden-attractions-A-Z/
glasshouses
The iconic Palm House, designed by Decimus Burton and engineered
by Richard Turner, was built between 1844 and 1848. A massive
restoration project in the 1980s has restored it to its former glory.
The Temperate House is said to be the largest surviving Victorian
glasshouse in the world.

Sefton Park, Liverpool L17 1AP.
Telephone: 0151 726 2415. Website: www.palmhouse.org.uk
Magnificent octagonal, domed palm house by Mackenzie & Moncur.

Sheffield Botanical Gardens, Clarkehouse Road, Sheffield S10 2LN.
Telephone: 0114 268 6001. Website: www.sbg.org.uk/index.asp
The two wings, known as 'Paxton's Pavilions', connecting the two
pavilions to the central one, have ridge-and-furrow roofs.

FURTHER READING

Campbell, Susan. *A History of Kitchen Gardening*. Frances Lincoln, 2005.

Desmond, Steven. 'The Richardson Inheritance', *Historic Garden* 6, summer 1993, pages 15–17.

Diestlekamp, E. 'Palaces of Light', *Country Life* 45, 1993.

Elliot, Brent. 'Changing Fashions in the Conservatory', *Country Life*, 30 June 1983.

Hix, John. *The Glasshouse*. Phaidon Press, 1996.

Hix, John. 'Richard Turner: Glass Master', *Architectural Review*, November 1972.

Kohlmaier, Georg, and von Sartory, Barna. *Houses of Glass: A Nineteenth-Century Building Type*. MIT Press, 1986.

Koppelkamm, Stefan. *Glasshouses and Wintergardens of the Nineteenth Century*. Granada, 1981.

Lemmon, Kenneth. *The Covered Garden*. London Museum Press, 1962.

Saudan-Skira, Sylvia, and Saudan, Michel. *Orangeries, Palaces of Glass – Their History and Development*. Evergreen, Cologne, 1998.

Woods, May, and Warren, Arete. *Glasshouses*. Aurum Press, 1988.

INDEX